International Baccalaureate

Option D

Medicines And Drugs

Revision Guide
(or if all else fails, read this)

2nd Edition
for exams 2009 onwards

Tony Brown

To Sarah, Hannah and Michael

This Booklet Is Not....

- Aimed at virgin I.B. chemists. I have assumed that you have (at the very least) sat in your option lessons, even if you didn't fully understand every word or perhaps you were looking out of the window? There is much assumed knowledge here.

- The answer to your dreams (if it is then you need to get a life.. quickly). It is merely another weapon in your armoury alongside teachers, books, and .. each other. Yes, strange as it may seem one of the best ways to learn is to talk to people and assuming that you don't talk to teachers try your friends. Discussing the merits of *in vivo* and *in vitro* testing in the lunch queue can impress the opposite sex *and* improve your grade.

Anyway, I hope it helps and good luck for the exams!

Topics by Page

I fear that I cannot (with the best will in the world) offer an 'after sales' e-mail tuition service. However if you would like to make any comments or suggestions for future productions or just have no-one else to talk to, then please feel free to e-mail me at brownt@godolphin.wilts.sch.uk

Introduction

The pharmaceuticals industry is the product of a collision between medicine, chemistry and international business. The sums of money involved are vast, and some aspects of the sector controversial. Yet the products that have been developed in the last couple of generations have transformed the way we live, improving the quality (and quantity) of life for much of the world's population.

This little booklet aims to provide a glimpse into this fascinating area of chemistry. It contains many complex organic structures. As the book says 'don't panic!' at the sight of these. With a bit of effort you will become familiar with their general shapes and be able to recognise them in an exam question. You will not be asked to draw the structure of heroin from memory!

All the money bits are quoted in US dollars, and a 'billion' is the US variety i.e. 10^9.

A 'heterocyclic' ring means one which contains elements apart from carbon.

1. Pharmaceutical Products

So what is a drug or medicine? It's actually quite a good question to ask.

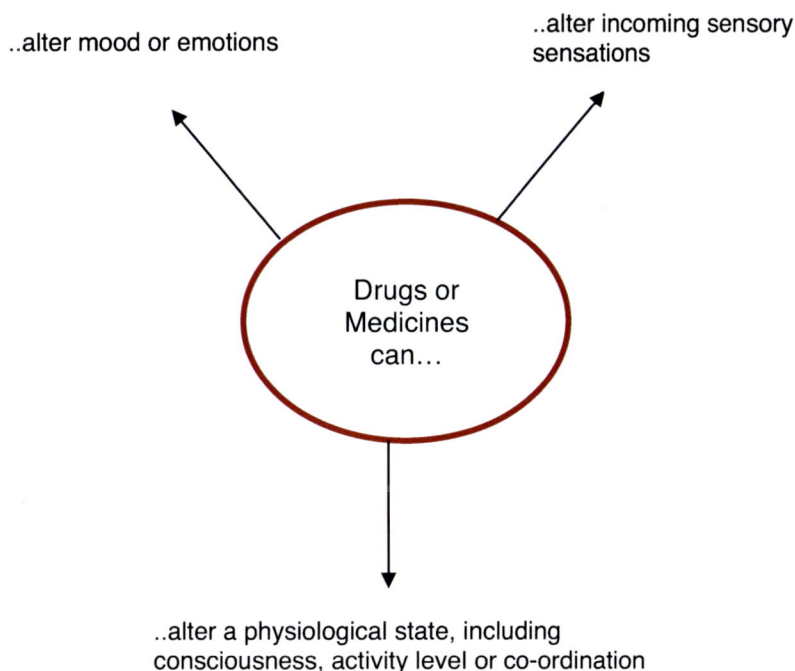

..alter mood or emotions

..alter incoming sensory sensations

Drugs or Medicines can…

..alter a physiological state, including consciousness, activity level or co-ordination

Within these three categories lie an enormous and fast growing range of substances. However there is a danger that we can get so fixated with our modern high technology approach to medicine that we forget how effective the body is at healing itself, often in extreme circumstances. A good doctor knows when to stand back and do nothing as well as when to intervene with drugs.

A powerful illustration of the body's self healing capacity is the *placebo effect*. It is well known in medicine that giving a patient a 'drug' which is in fact nothing of the sort, e.g. a sugar pill can still result in remarkable recoveries. This hints at our brain's ability to influence our physiology – if you really believe that you are going to get better you often do! The placebo effect is used by companies when testing the efficacy (effectiveness) of new drugs. Typically a 'blind' trial will take place where half of the patients are given the real drug and the other a placebo. The results are later compared. The most authoritative trials are 'double blind', meaning that neither the patients nor the administering doctors know which is which. It is likely that many of the sincere claims made for homeopathic medicine are based on the placebo effect.

Developing a New Drug
This is a long drawn out process and has many stages which I will summarise here.

1. A disease is first selected for new treatment.

2. Targets are identified along the 'disease process' which may be vulnerable to interference by a drug. Likely targets would be an enzyme or a gene that become involved at some stage in the disease. Perhaps these might be blocked in some way preventing the progress of the illness.

3. Potential 'lead molecules' are considered. These could be molecules already known to work in a similar area; they could be molecules designed by computer using an understanding of the detailed biochemistry involved (rational drug design); they could even be stumbled upon by random robotised screening of thousands and thousands of molecules (HL people see page 20).

4. The lead molecule is selected, with a couple chosen as 'reserve'. This decision is critical and depends on
   - which drugs seem most effective
   - which is easiest to manufacture
   - is there an advantage over existing drugs?
   - could it give a return on investment?

5. Preclinical Trials. This first involves testing the lead molecule in a laboratory environment, *in vitro* testing. The purpose is to test the potency of the molecule and its selectivity. After that, *in vivo* testing i.e. in living animals is carried out. This may be controversial but is essential and strictly regulated. Before it is given to people the effect of the drug on the body must be established. Are there side effects? The body can also have an effect on the drug. Molecules are frequently changed once they are inside you. This might inactivate them (or activate them if you are cunning) but it might lead to nasty side effects and these can't be discovered in any other way.

6. Phase I Trials. These are done on small numbers of healthy volunteers! Their aim is to assess the toxicology (poisonous effect) of the molecule. Is the drug safe? Can it be tolerated by the body? On occasions, and with their consent, drugs may be given to terminally ill patients who have no other alternative.

7. Phase II Trials. This is a clinical trial. Several hundred ill patients will be given either the drug or a placebo. During this stage the dosage needs to be decided upon and the way in which the drug might be administered (see below). At this point the pharmaceutical company will have to make expensive decisions about progressing or terminating the project.

8. Phase III Trials. Thousands of closely monitored patients are given the drug and the trial can last years. Massive amounts of data have to be collected to satisfy the various (and rightly strict) regulatory authorities. Even now it can all amount to nothing.

9. Dossiers are finally submitted to these regulatory bodies and if all is well (and it may not be) the drug is launched!

10. Phase IV Trials. Post launch monitoring of the drug. This may lead to new formulation, dosages or applications, or even *product extension*.

This entire process will take between 10 and 15 years! It will cost up to $500 million. At this point the company has not got a penny back, and it may happen that another company brings out something better in 6 months, or worse, that the drug proves to have unforeseen drawbacks.
To give you an idea of the money invested, one giant British pharmaceutical company, Glaxo-SmithKline, in 2007 had a research and development budget alone of $6.6 billion.

The modern procedure is thorough and exhaustive but there is always the chance that something might go wrong. In the 1950s the procedure was less thorough and exhaustive and something went badly wrong. *Thalidomide* was a new non addictive sedative and in much of Europe (but not the US) it was licensed for prescription from 1958 to 1963 (when it was withdrawn). It was given to women in the early stages of pregnancy as a treatment for 'morning sickness'. It worked well, but soon babies were being born dead or with terrible deformities of the limbs. Some 460 cases were recorded in the UK and 3000 in West Germany (as it was). Those who survived are now moving into graceful middle age. Legal actions followed, the company went bust and it was years and years before any compensation was forthcoming. The whole sorry episode was a watershed for the pharmaceuticals industry. Rules were tightened and nothing like it has happened since, but the ghost of Thalidomide sits on the board of every pharmaceuticals giant, looking straight into the eyes of the corporation lawyer.

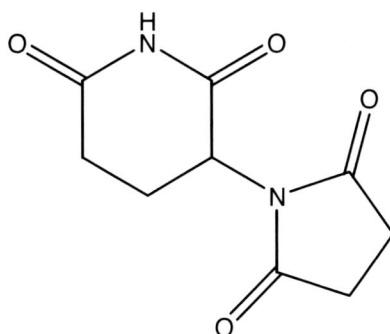

The infamous Thalidomide molecule, which was offered to author's mother when he was in the womb. She declined.

Although long since banned as a treatment for pregnancy the drug, under another name, is prescribed in South America for severe leprosy (a strange yet instructive example of product extension). Warnings against it being taken by pregnant women are predictably being ignored and the next generation of Thalidomide babies are still being born in the shanty towns of Brazil.

How Drugs are Administered
One of the questions that needs to be answered through all the long trials outlined above is how best to deliver the molecule to the patient. There are basically five methods:

- Oral. This could be a tablet or capsule or even a syrup. The drug would of course be subjected to the rigours of the digestive process. If stomach acid, for example, would deactivate the drug then this would not be the way to proceed. The advantage is obvious. It's the easiest way for the patient to take the drug and the patient could easily self-administer.

- Rectal. You are all intelligent people, use your imagination! Oddly there are cultural biases here which the companies need to consider before marketing any drug in a particular country. The British are very resistant to suppositories despite their efficiency. The Germans, on the other hand, use them all the time and happily buy this form of a medicine. Conclude from that what you will.

- Inhalation. Unless the drug can be absorbed through the lungs, or it is aimed at the lungs e.g. ventolin for asthma, then this is an unusual way of administering.

- Injections. The big advantages of injecting a drug is that it can be put directly where it is needed, rather than being spread all over the body. This reduces the dose necessary and reduces the chance that the body will in some way alter the molecular structure of the drug before it arrives at the right place. The disadvantages are that it usually (not always) requires medically trained staff to administer the drug and patients don't like it! Injections can made be into the blood stream, *intravenous*, which bypasses the acidic digestive system, quickens the arrival but still has the drawback of spreading out the dose. Alternatively they can be directed into body fat, *subcutaneous*, which is perfect for molecules which have a low solubility in water but which are soluble in fat. Finally, they can be straight into muscle tissue, *intramuscular*.

- Patches. These are a relatively new development, and are commonly used in administering decreasing amounts of nicotine in smokers trying to give up the habit. Some molecules can be absorbed directly through the skin barrier. Patches allow this to take place *gradually*. They are one of the best ways of introducing a drug at a continuous and controlled rate; everything else gives a sudden blast of the drug and then nothing for a period of time. They are also very acceptable to patients, a fact not lost on market conscious drugs companies!

Toxicology
Data also has to be collected on the toxicology of any new drug. A molecule that is therapeutic at one dose can kill you at another and it is handy to know at what point things change over!

LD_{50} values are frequently used to give an idea of how toxic a molecule might be. They tell you the *L*ethal *D*ose of a substance that kills off 50% of a population. Now clearly this has not been tested on humans (!) and so it will refer to mice or some other test animals. The units below are grams of chemical per kg of body mass of the test animal. It gives a very useful relative scale of toxicity but will not directly give you a 'safe' value for mice, still less humans where it is possible because of differences in biochemistry that even the relative toxicity will vary.

	LD_{50} g/kg
Aspirin	1.5
Nicotine	0.23
Caffeine	0.13
Botulin	3×10^{-11}

*Some examples of LD_{50} values. Remember
the smallest numbers are the most toxic!*

The other method, which is of more use to a doctor or an environmental scientist is *the maximum daily tolerance*, i.e. how much of a chemical can be taken into the body before undesirable symptoms occur. This is often related to the rate at which the body's biochemistry is able to get rid of the same agent. Such values will often have a 'safety factor' built in. These values may frequently be updated as more information comes in, particularly as the long term effects of a drug will become clearer only slowly. It is important that minimum doses of a drug are used whenever possible as the human body may start to become resistant to the effects of the molecule. This increased tolerance can then push doses up to unacceptably high levels to have the same efficacy.

One way in which a molecule can become toxic is through *side effects*. We should not be surprised that molecules designed to interfere with part of such a complex machine as the human body might possibly interfere with another unforeseen part of it. Thalidomide is the classic example of where the side effect was totally unacceptable and outweighed the beneficial impact of the drug. Yet it is not always so. Many drugs used in chemotherapy for cancer patients have terrible side effects of hair loss and nausea but are still given for their life saving potential. There is risk: benefit ratio that physicians must judge before deciding a treatment. One of the driving forces for new drug development is reduction of unwanted side effects relative to the current product.

2. Antacids

These may not be 'sexy'; they may not have complex and intriguing molecular structures but even humble inorganic compounds can qualify as a drug. The stomach, (as I'm sure you know) contains a dilute concentration of hydrochloric acid. If the pH strays too far from the ideal value then problems arise. Antacids are simply bases that neutralise excess acid. The following equations, show some of the common ingredients, particularly calcium and aluminium compounds. They are used as they are only sparingly soluble and hence will gently neutralise over a long period of time. Something like sodium hydroxide would be far too strong and too fast. These equations you need to know – sorry!

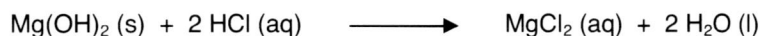

$$Mg(OH)_2 \text{ (s)} + 2\,HCl \text{ (aq)} \longrightarrow MgCl_2 \text{ (aq)} + 2\,H_2O \text{ (l)}$$

In the UK, magnesium hydroxide suspension has long been sold under the brand name 'milk of magnesia', but you can also buy an aluminium hydroxide equivalent:

$$Al(OH)_3 \text{ (s)} + 3\,HCl \text{ (aq)} \longrightarrow AlCl_3 \text{ (aq)} + 3\,H_2O \text{ (l)}$$

Then there is 'bicarbonate of soda', or as we ought to call it sodium hydrogen carbonate. Of course any treatment that produces a gas is going to make you burp or fart, but the laws of nature cannot be fought against!

$$NaHCO_3 \text{ (aq)} + HCl \text{ (aq)} \longrightarrow NaCl \text{ (aq)} + CO_2 \text{ (g)} + H_2O \text{ (l)}$$

Antacids are often combined with chemicals called *alginates*. Derived from algae these produce a gel-like layer preventing the acid in the stomach from rising into the oesophagus and causing 'heartburn'. Alginates are more commonly encountered as the thickening agents in ice cream!
To allow any gas produced to escape easily anti foaming agents may be added. An example is *dimethicone* which allows the gas bubbles to coalesce and be expelled. Dimethicone is a water resistant silicone polymer very similar to .. well you know what I mean.

3. Analgesics

An analgesic is a drug which relieves pain without the aid of sleep. They tend to fall into two categories; the powerful ones that you are given when you have an arm amputated and the mild ones that you take for a headache. Let's start with the second group.

Mild Analgesics
The first point to make is that these have a triad of properties. They are *analgesics* (pain relief), *antipyretics* (fever reduction) and *anti-inflammatories* (reduce swelling). It is thought they work at the site of the pain itself by blocking synthesis of chemicals called *prostaglandins*. These are local action hormones which, like many hormones, have a range of functions in the body. One of these may be in the action of pyrogens, chemicals which raise body temperature. Their inhibition would account for the antipyretic effect. Prostaglandins also seem to be responsible for the altering of signals going across the synapse junctions of nerves. The shape of an aspirin molecule seems to allow it to bind with

an enzyme prostaglandin cyclooxygenase and inhibit its production of prostaglandins. Without these molecules at the synapses, the messages to the brain can't be altered to read 'pain'.

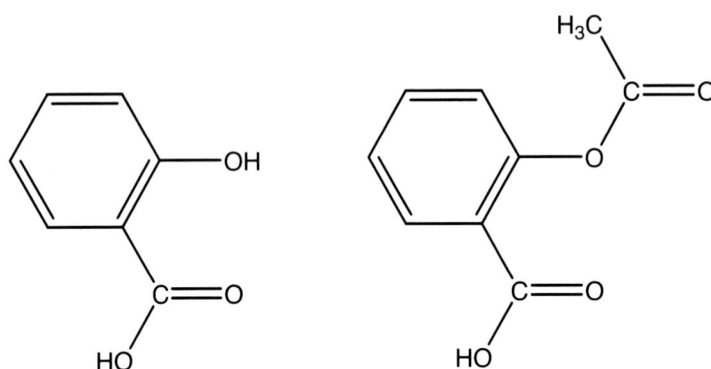

On the left salicylic acid and on the right, its derivative aspirin. Once out of favour, in recent years aspirin has staged a comeback being used for strokes and heart attacks – an excellent example of product extension.

Salicylic acid was isolated from Willow Bark in 1860 (used to treat pain since 1763). It was also found in a wild flower, *spiraea ulmaria*. It was effective but unpleasant to use, being too acidic. (You will see that the molecule contains both an alkanoic acid and a phenol group). In 1899 a German chemist Hoffman, working for the company Bayer, altered the structure of the molecule by adding an acetyl group. The first letter was added to the name of the flower and aspirin was born. For 50 years it had no rivals, but there were problems.

- The acidity of the molecule is still significant and can lead to stomach ulcers and hence stomach bleeding if used in excess.
- It is an anti-coagulant, which means it can potentially cause problems of internal bleeding.
- There can be allergic reactions.
- In children it can induce Reye's Syndrome – a potentially fatal liver and brain disorder.

As a result of the above, aspirin is no longer the analgesic of choice with children under twelve. On the other hand, its blood thinning properties have life saving potential for victims of heart attacks and strokes. Indeed it has just been reported as being active against some cancers.

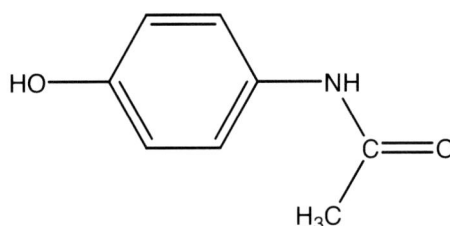

Paracetamol (acetaminophen) has none of the problems of aspirin as long as the correct dose is used.

Paracetamol has a similar shape to aspirin which suggests a similar mechanism of operation. It has become the most popular analgesic in the world as, at the correct dose, it has none of the side effects of aspirin. However if doses of paracetamol are exceeded it can be a killer, inducing massive liver damage. Paracetamol overdoses are often used as an instrument of suicide. Failed attempts can lead to a catalogue of medical problems centred around the liver. On a brighter note paracetamol in syrup form is often used to successfully reduce childhood fevers.

Strong Analgesics

These molecules work in a totally different way to their milder cousins. They go straight to the brain. Here they find specific chemical receptors that receive pain messages. The analgesic molecules all have a structure that allows them to bind with, and hence block, these receptors, stopping the transmission of pain as they do so.

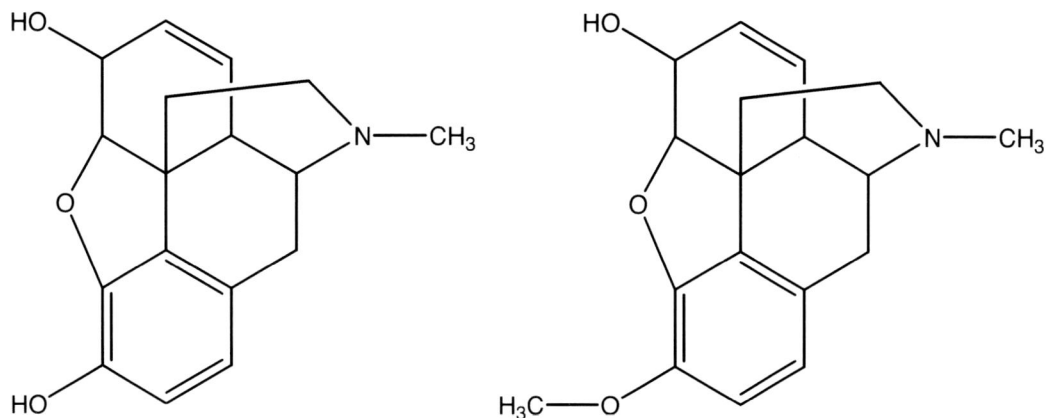

Morphine (left) and Codeine. Note the almost identical three dimensional molecular shapes.

Strong analgesics are almost all related to morphine which itself was extracted from the opium poppy. The family is called the opium alkaloids and they have very similar molecular shape. Codeine (see above) differs from morphine only by removing a hydrogen from one of the alcohol groups and replacing it by a methyl group (-CH₃).

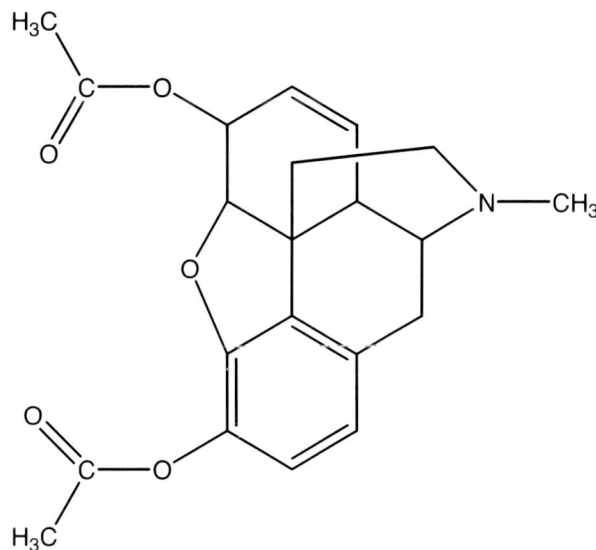

Diamorphine or Heroin – a synthetic derivative of morphine and one of the strongest analgesics known.

For HL only - Diacetylmorphine (heroin, see above) replaces the hydrogens from both alcohol groups with, once again, those acetyl (-COCH₃) groups. It is also called diamorphine for short.

Removal of the two –OH groups makes heroin much less soluble in water, but more soluble in fatty tissue. The result is that heroin needs to be injected directly into the blood stream, but is able to pass through the blood-brain barrier much more easily than morphine. The effects of the drug are therefore accelerated and intensified but last for a shorter time.

Molecules like heroin or morphine are incredibly strong analgesics, but there is one overwhelming problem with opiates, *addiction*. So serious is this that heroin has only limited analgesic use and even morphine cannot be used for long periods of time. The brain produces its own pain killers called *endorphins* which appear to block the same receptors as do the opiates. The discovery of these endorphins, in 1979, explained the long known phenomena that many people under great trauma, in war or in a car accident for example, feel little pain despite terrible injuries. The brain floods these receptors with endorphins. It seems that the morphine and the others suppress the production of these natural molecules and that even under normal conditions a low level of endorphins is necessary for proper brain activity. When a heroin addict suffers horrible withdrawal symptoms it might be the behaviour of the body without any endorphins at all. Perhaps in the future, synthetic endorphins could be used as major analgesics without the addictive side effect. The social problems of heroin addiction are known to us all.

It is interesting to note a correlation between the addictive risk and ability to suppress pain of the opiate; codeine least, heroin most.

4. Depressants

To start on a confusing note, these drugs are often referred to as 'anti-depressants' as they can be used to combat depression. Their effects can be varied and its all a matter of dosage.

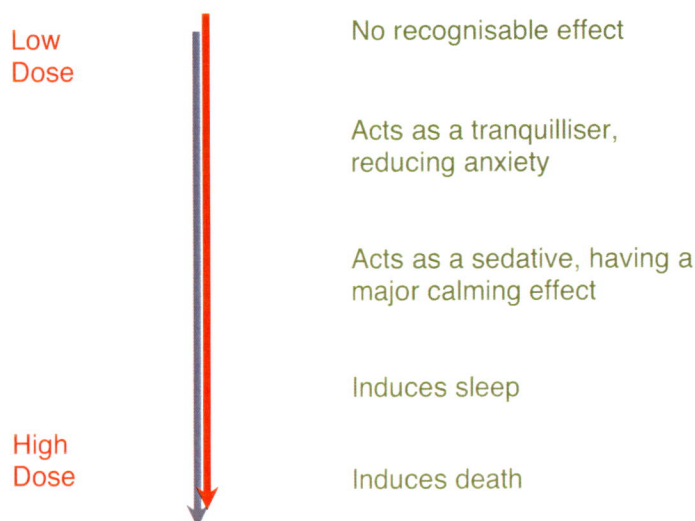

Low Dose — No recognisable effect

Acts as a tranquilliser, reducing anxiety

Acts as a sedative, having a major calming effect

Induces sleep

High Dose — Induces death

Ethanol
Surprisingly ethanol is a mild depressant, although ironically in moderate doses it appears to have the *opposite* effect, making people more lively and uninhibited! This is an example of a side effect of a molecule masking the main effect. Of course as it is drunk socially it is by far

and away the most significant drug taken by most adults, and the problems are well documented.

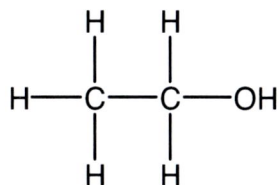

$$H-C-C-OH$$

Ethanol. This unassuming little molecule has much to answer for.

The effects of drinking can be physiological, social and economic. Although most drinking is fine and great fun the serious side to alcohol abuse is massive and should not be underestimated. It is estimated that in the USA alone there are over 10 million alcoholics. In some societies the problem is much worse than that. No doubt many of you reading this will have personal knowledge of some aspect of alcohol abuse.

Physiological Effects	Social and Economic Consequences
• Reduction in inhibitions	• Violent behaviour to family or strangers
• Short term reduction in reaction speed	• Increase in car accidents
• Short term hangover	• Absenteeism from work
• Long term liver (and much other) damage	• Cost of intensive medical care

The amount of alcohol that you can safely drink depends on your body mass and how tolerant your body is, i.e. how regularly you drink. However some approximate figures make interesting reading. (For the record, you reduce your blood level by about 0.015% per hour).

➤ At a blood level of 0.05% alcohol, you will have reduced co-ordination and lowered alertness.

➤ At 0.1% your reaction time has slowed by a quarter.

➤ At 0.25% you will be staggering and dizzy.

➤ At 0.4% you will be deeply unconscious and your body temperature will be falling.

➤ At 0.5% you will probably be dead.

In my own country, the UK, there has been a dramatic change in the way drink driving is perceived. For my parents' generation it was socially acceptable, even a bit of a laugh, but no more. In part this is due to the police. Most police forces in the world now breathalyse drivers on suspicion of drinking and sometimes even randomly.

The older style of breathalyser involved a plastic bag into which you blew, your breath passing over some orange crystals of *potassium dichromate*. You may recall (if you don't, do some revision!) that any ethanol present will be oxidised to ethanal and then ethanoic acid. The crystals turn green as a result.

A more modern roadside device uses infra red light to detect the ethanol. These are called *intoximeters*. HL students will have come across infra red spectroscopy in their course. The basic idea is that IR light causes covalent bonds to vibrate. The C-O bond in ethanol vibrates strongly at a known frequency. These machines determine the degree of IR absorption and hence calculate the amount of ethanol present in the breath.
However to get a prosecution most countries require a blood or urine test to measure the % alcohol content. This requires bigger equipment and is probably going to be done in a police station and not by the roadside. These work by *gas chromatography*. In brief, a long (25m), thin tube with an inert material inside has the sample passed through under pressure. The components of the sample separate out and are then identified.

Other Depressants

The only three we need mention here are from a class called *benzodiazepenes* and they include household names such as valium® and prozac®. Once again they are all similar in structure. As a class, the benzodiazpenes were developed in the 1960s replacing barbiturates which were used all too often as an instrument of suicide.

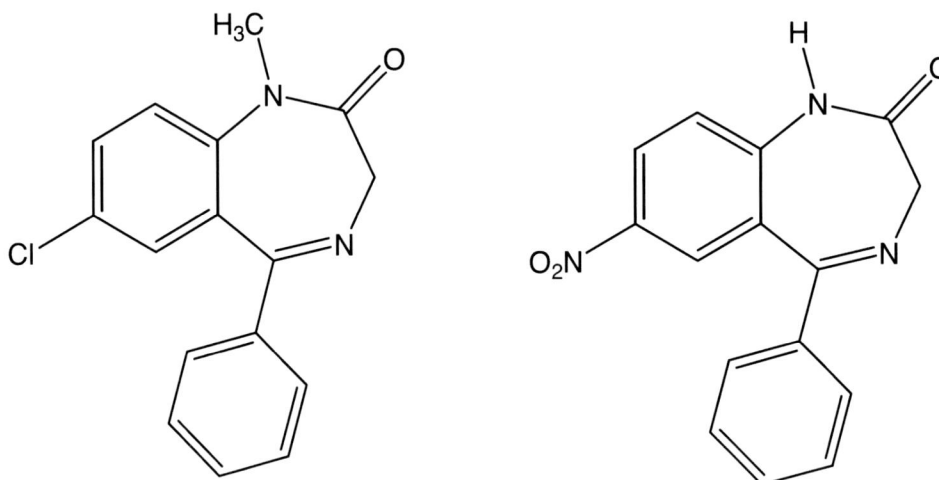

Diazepam (Valium ®) and Nitrazapam (Mogadon®). The latter has a nitro group on one of the benzene rings and a hydrogen on the heterocyclic ring.

These frequently used tranquillisers are controversial and in the past may have been over prescribed by doctors. They may become addictive. Notice that yet again all three structures are very similar.

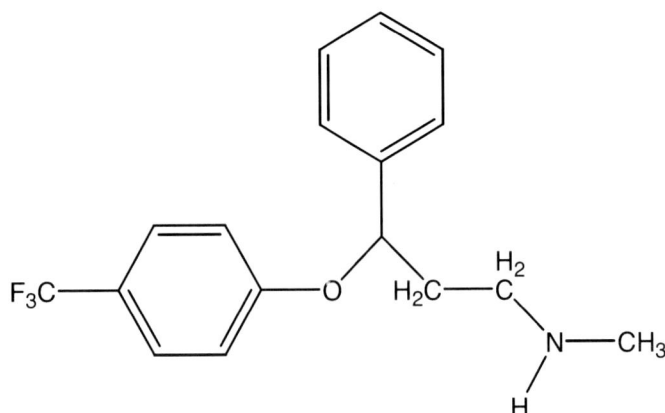

Fluoxetine Hydrochloride, better known as Prozac®. It differs from the two above in that the heterocyclic ring has 'burst' and that a – CF₃ group is now attached to the benzene.

Benzodiazapenes have a **synergistic effect** with ethanol. As they are both depressants you might expect the effect of having the two together as being cumulative. In fact the combination is far, far more effective than either drug singly. The combination is better thought of as a multiplication of their effects and this is the synergistic effect. This is why tranquillisers and alcohol together are so highly dangerous. Like the opiates, the benzodiazapenes work on chemical receptors in the brain. They bind to a special protein which is found at the synapse of nerve junctions. This indirectly results in the widening of the synapse gap preventing the nerve cell from producing a signal, reducing anxiety. Ethanol works in a similar manner, on a different part of the same protein. Using the two together can result in a neural shutdown. Another (very different) synergistic effect of ethanol is with aspirin; taken together there is a real danger of stomach bleeding.

5. Stimulants

These are molecules that increase alertness and give you a greater sensitivity to external stimuli. Your mental processes may speed up, you may feel elated or possibly anxious. In short they do the opposite of the depressants above.

Amphetamine and Adrenaline
These two illustrate a common tendency in medicines for a synthetic drug to mimic the structure of a naturally occurring molecule. We have already seen this with opiates and endorphins. Amphetamine is a (primary) amine having a $-NH_2$ group. It is one of a number of *sympathomimetic* amines which mimic the chemical behaviour of hormones in the nervous system. Caffeine (below) is another such amine.

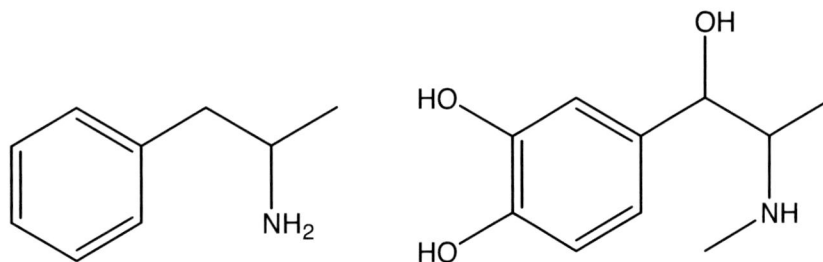

Amphetamine (left) and Adrenaline (right) – similarly shaped 'backbones'.

Adrenaline is a naturally occurring hormone and stimulant. It is released when we are under stress and invokes a range of responses from the body including increased heartbeat, dilation of pupils, sweating, diversion of blood to muscles and decreased blood clotting time. However it has three –OH groups which make it water soluble but fat insoluble. The result is that is unable to pass through the blood-brain barrier. Variations of adrenaline are therefore produced in situ in the brain. One of these is called norepinephrine.

Amphetamine on the other hand, has no such problems. It can pass straight into the brain where it mimics norepinephrine. Norepinephrine is a neurotransmitter and its job is to send signals to the brain by binding with neural proteins. As always it will only fit into specific sites and these are to be found in the parts of the brain responsible for alertness and emotion.

When amphetamines are introduced, the similarity is so strong that the drug will actually replace norepinephrine in its storage sites. This results in a flood of displaced norepinephrine molecules that bind to all the neural proteins and trigger lots of signals - hence a feeling of euphoria.

Both molecules are based on the framework of phenyl ethyl amine i.e. a benzene ring with a two carbon chain and an amine group at the end.

Nicotine

Nicotine is, of course, present in tobacco, in fact about 5 mg in each cigarette, although only between 0.2 and 3.5 mg are actually absorbed. Once in the body it quickly reaches the central nervous system where it has several effects including a reduction in urine output (no, really!) and a lowering of reflex times. The knee jerk reaction is significantly slower in smokers.

Short Term Effects	Long Term Effects
• Increased heart rate and blood pressure	• Increased risk of heart disease
• Reduction in urine output	• Coronary Thrombosis
• Decrease in reflex times	• Peptic Ulcers

Long term, things get much more serious as the table above indicates. Remember that nicotine is just one of many chemicals inhaled when smoking and from the others any number of ailments can be acquired. Lung cancer is the most obvious.

Nicotine is also used as an agricultural insecticide – a thought to ponder on when next reaching for a cigarette!

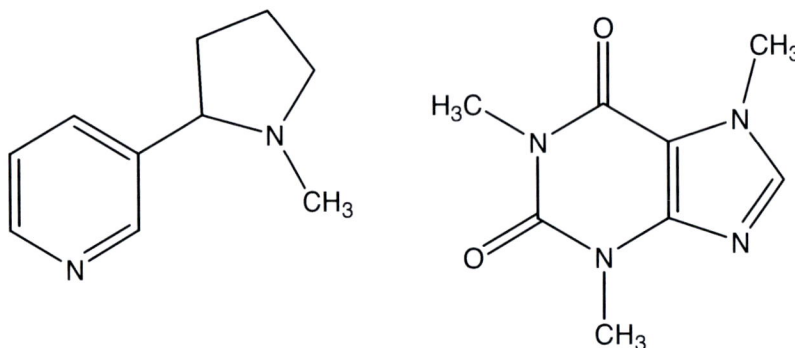

Nicotine (left) and Caffeine, both tertiary amines and both stimulants

Nicotine is what is called a tertiary amine. This means there is (at least) one nitrogen atom which has three carbon fragments coming from it, so for nicotine it is the N in the pentagon with the methyl group (-CH_3) coming of it.

Caffeine has no less than three tertiary amine groups and has a passing resemblance to nicotine. It is of course the stimulant that is found in tea, coffee and cola and can promote mild dependence. It is also a mild diuretic, which means it does the opposite of nicotine and encourages the production of urine. A cup of coffee may contain 100 mg of the drug and for those who are not used to it, four cups a day may have a noticeable effect on behaviour, in particular an increase in *anxiety* and problems with sleeping *(insomnia)*.

Caffeine is known as a respiratory stimulant. Hence it increases the rate of respiration and temporarily gives the body more energy. How does it work? Well it is all rather cunning. As any biochemists out there will know, the body's 'energy molecule' is called ATP (adenosine tri-phosphate you will recall). Breakdown of ATP to its relative ADP releases energy and that is what respiration is all about. However, there is an enzyme, this time called *phospho-diesterase*, which binds with the ATP and prevents its breakdown – hence storing its energy.

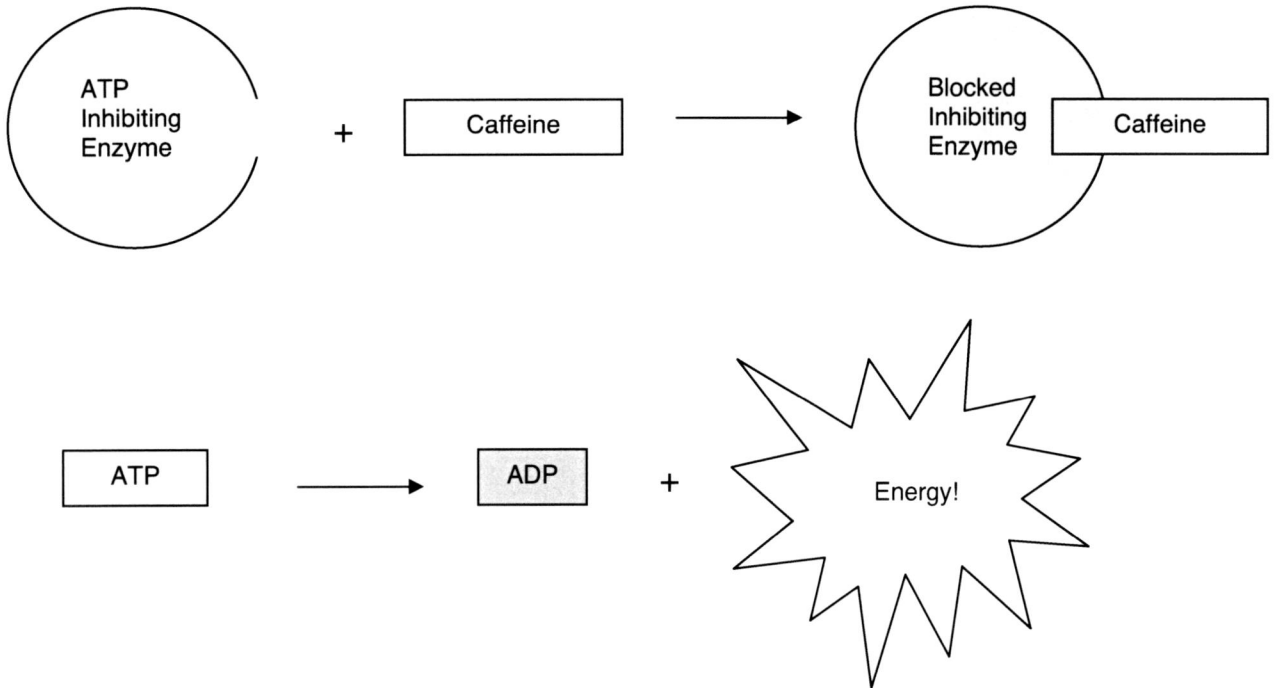

The caffeine molecule mimics the shape of ATP and binds to this enzyme, so preventing the inhibition of the ATP and allowing the release of extra energy.

6. Antibacterials

In our syllabus we are only concerned with penicillins (which is a pity really as there is so much more to the subject). They were not the first drugs taken to cure bacterial infections, but they were the first naturally occurring ones. Penicillins are a wide class of similar molecules, the first of which were found in moulds. Why should moulds produce these molecules? The obvious answer is to kill off local bacteria and reduce the competition for food from other species in their own 'patch'.

The story starts, as I guess everyone knows, in 1928, in a room at St Mary's Hospital, University of London where a young Scot, Alexander Fleming, was doing research on bacteria. One morning he noticed that some of the bacterial colonies he had been growing had died off where something had blown onto his petri dish. That 'something', which might have come in through an open window, was penicillin. Fleming's achievement was not to ignore his apparent setback, but to set out to identify what had killed the bacteria. However he was not able to isolate the penicillin in sufficient amounts to do meaningful experiments. That was not done until 1940, when Howard Florey and Ernst Chain, working at Oxford University, managed to purify the drug and allow it to be used clinically, just in time for much of WW II. All three received the Nobel Prize in 1945.

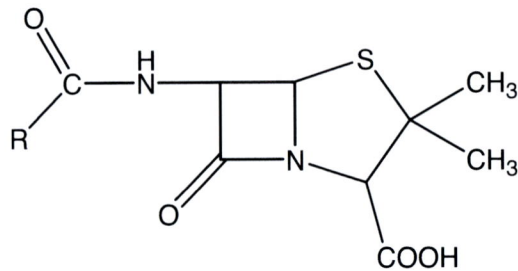

The generalised Penicillin structure. With its adjacent square and pentagon, with the heterocyclic (in the ring) nitrogen and sulphur, it is very distinctive.

Penicillin's mode of action is well understood. Bacteria have a different structure to their cells than mammals, and one of the differences is the cell wall present in bacteria. It is made up of polymers called mucoproteins. To form a networked wall these protein chains need to cross-link, and an enzyme exists to help them do this, called *peptidoglycan transpeptidase*. Penicillins inhibit this enzyme, consequently new cell wall cannot be made and the internal pressures within the cell build up.

HL only. The key to penicillin action is the 'square' heterocylic ring, called a **beta-lactam ring**.

This contains an amide group, but because the ring is so small the substantial bond strain makes the amide very reactive. In the presence of the *peptidoglycan transpeptidase* the ring breaks and a covalent bond is formed between it and the penicillin molecule, inhibiting its action. Isn't that clever?

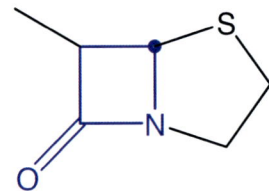

Eventually the bacterium bursts open and dies. Mammalian cells have a different structure and the targeted enzyme does not exist. Neither does it exist in viruses, and so penicillins are useless against viral infections, a point to remember.

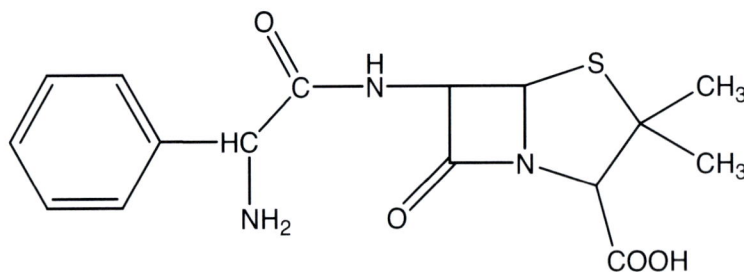

Ampicillin, one of the most widely used penicillins.

However, in living systems things never stand still. With the widespread use of penicillins bacteria were evolving to combat them. Some strains started producing new enzymes, called rather simply *penicillinases* to counter the drugs. *Penicillinases* attack the square ring in the structure (the beta-lactam ring) degrading the molecule and preventing it inhibiting the formation of new cell wall.

In the earliest penicillin, the –R group above was a benzene ring attached to a CH_2, i.e. $C_6H_5CH_2$- It was found that by altering the side chain, and also slightly changing the sulphur ring, variants could be made which were still active against these *pencillinase* producing bacteria. The variants were called *cephalosporins* and much modern research centres around the improvement of these molecules. Drug resistance is a real problem for doctors and chemists alike. For each move the pharmaceutical chemist makes in changing the molecular structure of the drug, nature rapidly counters by developing new enzymes and defences against it. Things are made worse by the over exposure of some antibiotics to the bacteria. Penicillins are known as *broad spectrum* antibiotics (in contrast to narrow spectrum), which means that they are effective against a wide range of bacteria and have been used pretty indiscriminately over the years. The fact is that antibiotics have in many countries been prescribed by doctors when not necessary or even downright useless, such as against viral infections. This encourages surviving bacteria to develop biochemical countermeasures and become resistant. This is why cephalosporins are so important. Already for some 'super bacteria' we are almost out of effective antibiotics and whilst it may be a little over dramatic to say we will ever go back to the pre-antibiotic age, it may be true to say that combating bacterial infections is going to become increasingly difficult in the years to come.

The situation is worsened still further by the habit of using some antibiotics as a supplement to animal feedstock on farms. The idea is to improve the health, and hence the productivity, of farm animals, but there is now considerable evidence to suggest that this practice is substantially contributing towards bacterial resistance.

7. Antivirals

A bacterium is a complete living unit – a single cell. It may be simple but within its structure it has a wide range of biochemical 'machinery' which can do all that is needed to keep it alive and to reproduce itself. Controlling and instructing this 'machinery' is the bacterial DNA housed in the cell nucleus. The whole thing is like an entry level starter kit for life.

A virus is nothing of the sort. It contains DNA all right (protected by a protein case), but none of the necessary machinery. So it has to hijack the machinery from another cell if it is to, for example, replicate. Whether this disqualifies viruses from being truly 'alive' is a moot point. The virus will stick to the outside of the cell, inject its own DNA which then inserts itself to the host DNA, in effect reprogramming the host cell to make lots of baby viruses. These then, in the manner of hatching chicks, break through the cell wall and escape to infect more cells. A bit of a hum drum existence you might think, yet a chain reaction like this can be fatal to the host whether it is a bacterium or a blue whale.

Viruses therefore pose particular problems for pharmaceutical chemists, problems which have meant that the field of anti-viral drugs lies far behind that of anti-bacterials. It is the principle of *selective toxicity* that allows drugs to work. This means they inhibit some process essential to the pathogen but absent in the host, the action of penicillins is a good example. However, as viruses use the processes of the host cell for much of what they do selective toxicity is far harder. Killing the virus is easy, but keeping the patient alive at the same time is not!

There are three possible approaches I outline below. Now this is quite subtle stuff, so if you know any biochemistry it will make things a bit clearer! If you don't, then I wouldn't worry about the details I describe.

1. The Trojan Horse. The virus infected cell is programmed to create lots of new viral genetic material. This is done by a host enzyme, *DNA-polymerase*, which zips down the infected DNA collecting genetic fragments together and making a new copy. However an anti-viral drug is introduced which is structurally similar to one of these genetic fragments. This is swept up by the *DNA-polymerase*, and joins the DNA chain. But it is a Trojan Horse and is unable to continue the chain and the replication is stopped in its

tracks! The selectivity arises as before this can occur the drug has first to be 'activated' in the cell by an enzyme, and this is a viral enzyme not a host one. So healthy cells are unaffected.

2. The Retrovirus inhibitors. A *retrovirus* is one that contains, not DNA, but RNA. Ordinarily the RNA is injected into the host cell, and acts as a template for a complementary DNA chain to be created (the reverse of what normally happens). The viral enzyme that helps this is *reverse-transcriptase*. The drug is introduced and inhibits this enzyme and prevents the formation of the viral DNA.

3. Blunting the scissors. Once the new baby viruses have been created within the infected cells they need to escape to infect other cells. To do this they have an enzyme (*neuraminidase* if you really want to know) which in effect cuts open the host cell wall like a pair of scissors. All we have to do is to introduce the ever present inhibitor molecule, and the viruses will be stuck within, forever harmless. This type of drug has been developed using computer modelling.

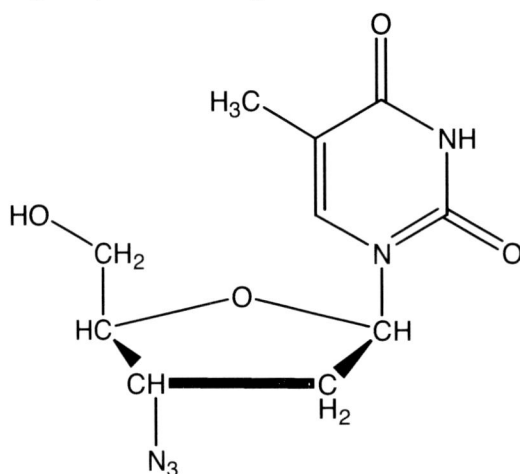

AZT (Azidothymadine) is the best known anti AIDS drug. It is a reverse transcriptase inhibitor.

AIDS (Acquired Immune Deficiency Syndrome) develops from HIV (human immunodeficiency virus) which is a retrovirus. Specific proteins on HIV bind to a receptor protein on certain white blood cells, called T cells destroying the immune system. It can be treated with reverse transcriptase inhibitors (see 2 above) like AZT, but the virus mutates quickly and 'learns' to cope with these. One way forward has been to use several drugs simultaneously, which seems to overcome the problems of mutations. Neuraminidase inhibitors (see 3 above) are potentially very exciting as the viral 'scissors' enzyme cannot mutate as it must cut the host protein cell wall. Hence it is a fixed and unchanging target for an attacking drug molecule.

This marks the (welcome) end of this option for all SL chemists. However not for you HL types, oh no! You have hardly begun; thirsting for more; craving for deeper knowledge and understanding. So hold onto your hats, here we go...

18

8. Drug Action (HL)

Thus far we have met a never ending stream of molecules which have 'just the right shape' to inhibit an enzyme. Well, you HL people know a thing or two about molecular shape, and will also appreciate that the three dimensional arrangement of functional groups in a molecule can be vital. We'll come to chirality in a moment, but first let's look at **cis-trans** (geometrical) isomerism in a new setting. For alkenes, you will recall, the inability to rotate groups around a C=C bond results in these two isomers existing; cis, on the same side and trans, opposite. Well the same thing can happen in inorganic transition metal complexes.

Trans and cis diamminedichloro platinum (II) complexes. The one on the right, 'cisplatin', has saved thousands of lives.

Here we have two platinum complexes and they are as much cis-trans isomers as anything you will find in organic chemistry. The *stereochemistry* of the complex is central to their medical efficacy. The cis form is abbreviated to cisplatin and since 1978 has been used as a major weapon against a range of cancers. The drug is given in salt solution (this keeps the chlorine ligands attached) and makes its way into the cell nucleus. Once there, the chlorines get removed by water molecules. As the complex ion gets near DNA, nitrogen atoms on some of the base pairs form co-ordinate bonds with the platinum. The cis isomer is able to do this simultaneously with two consecutive base pairs in the DNA chain (the trans isomer could not do this). This pulls the base pairs together and introduces a 'kink' on the helix. This kink prevents the replication of the DNA (*DNA polymerase* again).

Chirality occurs almost everywhere you look in biochemistry. Drug molecules have to fit into three dimensional binding sites or receptors and almost inevitably one isomer will fit and the other will not.

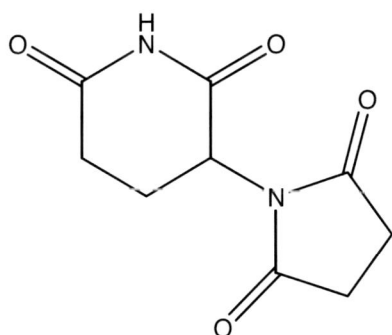

We can now take another look at the thalidomide molecule mentioned earlier in the booklet. The heterocyclic nitrogen in the *hexagon* is the atom of interest, one might almost say the culprit. It is tetrahedral, and has four different groups coming from it – one hydrogen, two asymmetric sides of the ring and a lone pair of electrons. This means it is a chiral centre and the molecule can exist in two enantiomeric forms.

As it happened, one of the enantiomers was successful in alleviating the morning sickness for which the drug was sold, but the other, which had no beneficial effect whatsoever, caused the birth deformities already discussed.

9. Drug Design (HL)

The synthetic route of many drugs often results in the formation of two (or more, if there is more than one chiral centre!) enantiomers, or racemic mixtures. Improved synthesis can result in a stereospecific product but it might well be a much more expensive way of making the drug. Even then there can still be problems. Drugs are often altered *once in the body*, and a single isomer might well be made back into a racemic mixture.

Many modern drug syntheses make use of **chiral auxiliaries**. These are added chiral molecules that temporarily bond to the non chiral reactant species and force it to react in a stereospecific way. After this has happened the auxiliary will detach itself leaving behind only the one enantiomer of the product molecule. If no auxiliary had been present then a racemic mixture would have resulted. They are analogous to surface catalysts, apart from that they may not always return to their original form at the end. This is a new and fast moving area of synthetic research. Such molecules have been used in the synthesis of one of the most recent anti-cancer drugs, *taxol*. Taxol is a complex multi-ringed molecule, isolated from a very rare tree, the Pacific Yew. It is exciting as it works against certain cancers in a manner unlike any other drug (it inhibits cell mitosis). It was not until 1994 that a (very complex) synthesis using a chiral auxiliary was reported and the drug approved against breast cancer.

Combinatorial Chemistry

In the section on anti-viral drugs I mentioned that the technique of computer modelling has been used to design active molecules from first principles. This is very exciting and is becoming more common as our understanding of biochemistry improves. However it is not the only way of finding new drugs. Trial and error has always been vital but when you're working 'blind' it can be a laborious process.

In recent years a method of automating 'trial and error' has been developed, called *combinatorial chemistry*. Using this technique, thousands of molecules can be synthesised very rapidly, and in sufficient quantities for in vitro (test tube) tests to be done to determine any activity against, for example, a target enzyme. To explain how it works let us take the combination of amino acids to make peptides. This variation of combinatorial chemistry is called *mix and split*. The example below is simplified in terms of the number of amino acids used.

Stage 1: each of the three amino acids present – shown by the symbols – is attached to very small (0.1 mm across) resin beads. Excess amino acid is washed away.

Stage 2: The three products from stage 1 are now mixed and then split into three separate containers. Each container is then exposed to an excess of one of the three amino acids. This results in all combinations of dipeptides (2 joined amino acids) being formed. Once again the excess reactant is washed away.

Stage three: Once more the three containers are mixed and once more they are split into three. As before each container is exposed to an excess of one of the three amino acids, which after the reaction is washed away. At this point we will have tri-peptides, and all of the 27 possible structures will have been made.

There is no need to stop there, and quite quickly a *combinatorial library* of thousands of different structures will have been created. Note that a solid phase is being used as a base upon which the reactions take place. Once you have got the peptides as long as required it is a relatively simple step to detach them from the resin bead. This technique is now being used by pharmaceutical companies to synthesise a wide range of potentially useful molecules. It is now fully automated.

Container One reacts with:	Container Two reacts with:	Container Three reacts with:

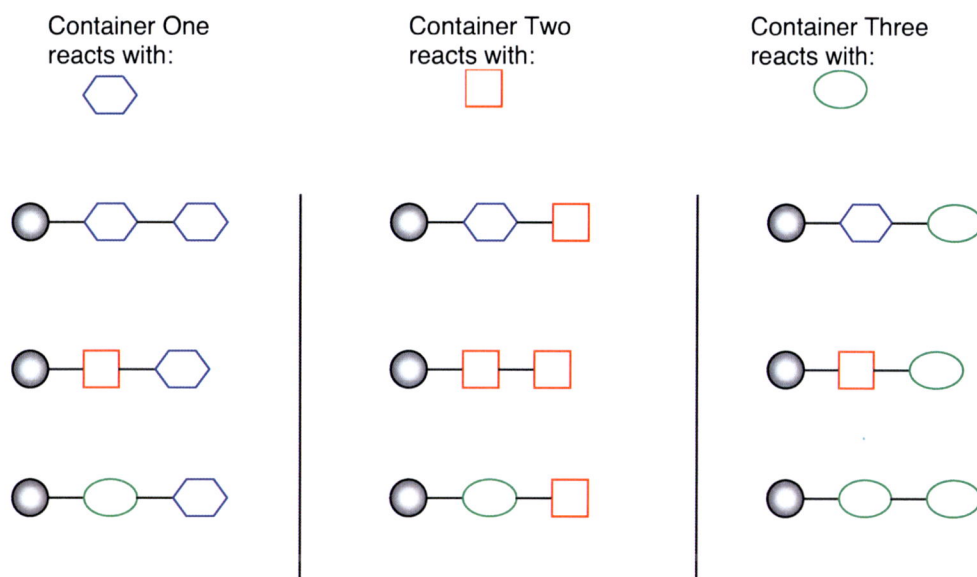

10. Mind-altering Drugs (HL)

Lysergic Acid Diethylamide –better known as LSD, or as The Beatles put it, 'Lucy in the Sky with Diamonds'

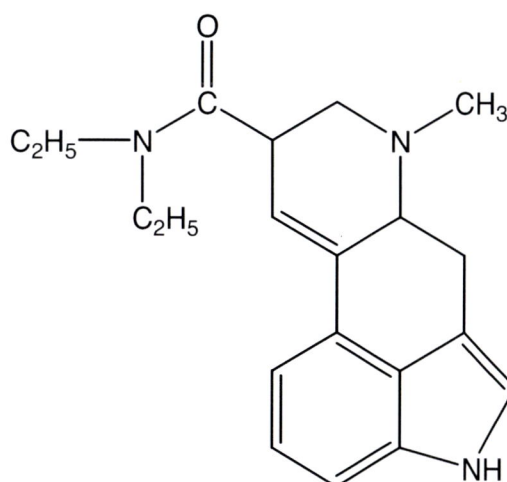

Unlike Heroin or Cocaine, or even Cannabis, LSD has no medical use – it is simply used as a narcotic, or mind altering drug better called an *hallucinogen*.   What it does is to alter our perception of what we are experiencing. This might be pleasurable but it might also be very frightening. There is also the real risk of doing something dangerous whilst under its influence. It was discovered by chance by a Swiss chemist in 1943 who administered himself an exceptionally high dose!

The bottom two rings of the molecule are together called an *indole ring* and are also to be found in other hallucinogenic drugs.

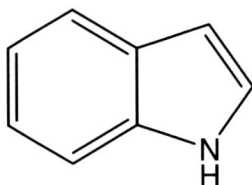

The indole ring appears intact in psilocybin and as a 'shadow' in mescaline, both of which are hallucinogens, and shows that they are all chemically related.

These two drugs, like so many others, are extracted from nature, psilocybin from certain fungi and mescaline, for long used by South American Indians, in a particular cactus plant. The symptoms are broadly similar to LSD, altered perception leading to colour hallicination, a distorted sense of time and often feelings of anxiety.

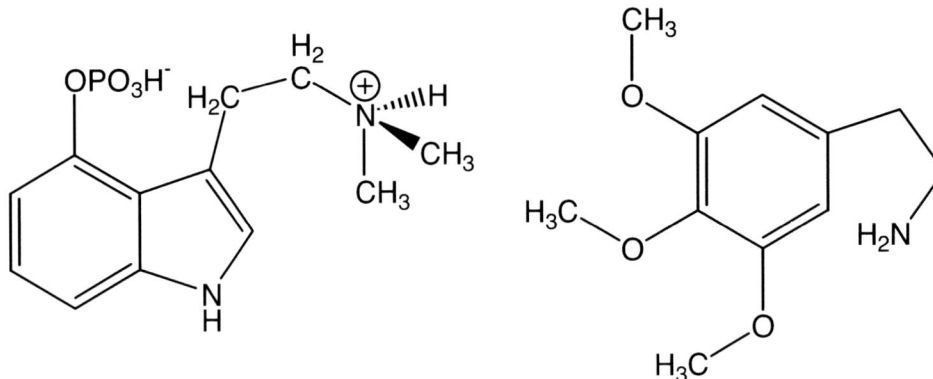

Psilocybin (left) and mescaline.

Cannabis

Cannabis is a weed, and when dried it is called marijuana. The active chemical is largely tetrahydrocannibol (THC) which unlike those above is not based around an indole ring.

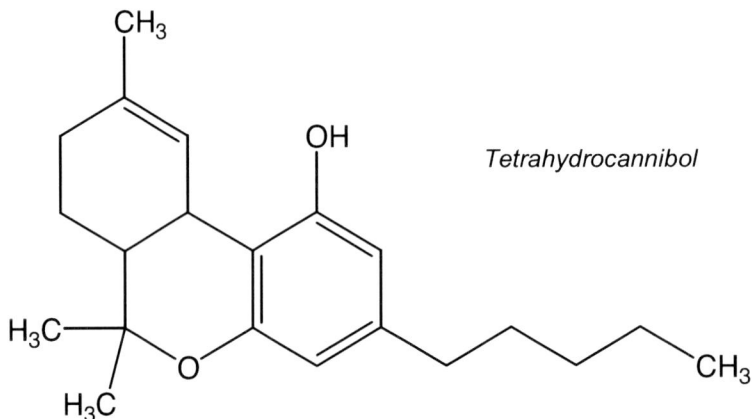

Tetrahydrocannibol

It is the most popular recreational drug in use after ethanol, but in many countries its use is illegal. The wisdom of this illegality has been debated over many years and different countries and indeed cultures have justified the ban in varied ways. A few countries, notably Holland, have legalised its use albeit under strict regulation. In other countries an argument is raging. Nor is the debate only about recreational use. There is some evidence to support claims that cannabis has some legitimate medical uses and should be legalised for the treatment of these alone. One of its effects is to impair some motor functions, but for people who suffer from Parkinson's Disease where they have little control over these functions it is claimed that cannabis can have a beneficial effect in treating the symptoms.

Some of the oft quoted arguments on both sides of the legalisation argument are given below.

- It is claimed that cannabis is addictive – this is contested.

- It is claimed that cannabis use leads on to harder drug use such as cocaine or heroin – the problem here is to know whether this is due to the cannabis inducing people to try other substances or whether heroin users would automatically start with cannabis due to its easy availability.

- It is claimed that cannabis is toxic – there are studies into this and there may well be toxic effects of the drug. Of course ethanol is also toxic, but there is no call to ban that.

- It is claimed that if cannabis was legalised then demands might be made for legalisation of other drugs. The 'thin end of the wedge'.

- It is claimed that cannabis should be legalised to remove the profits from criminals and to ensure that people are actually getting the correct drug at a safe dose. What is sold on the street is uncontrolled and can bear little resemblance to what is 'advertised'. Also with purity varying, the effects of a 'trip' are hard to predict.

Test Yourself Questions

Reading or even scribbling over a revision guide is all well and good but you need to practice questions. Use these to test yourself once you have studied the booklet. Do them as quickly as you reasonably can and do NOT cheat! Once you have finished, go back, find out the answers and mark how well you have done. Remember that one mark available means one point to be included, so use this as a guide.

Questions for both HL and SL

Q1 (a) Give three effects of a molecule on the body, any of which would allow it to be called a drug. [3]

1...

2...

3...

(b) Give a *brief* account of the process for developing and testing new drugs. Mention four distinct stages. [4]

....

....

....

....

....

....

(c) There are several ways of administering drugs. Choose *three* ways and for each, mention *one* advantage of using that particular method. [6]

1st...

....

2nd...

....

3rd...

....

Q2 Magnesium hydroxide, $Mg(OH)_2$, can be used as an antacid. A bottle of this may also contain dimethicone and an alginate additive.

(a) What does an antacid do? [1]

....

(b) Write a balanced equation, with state symbols for the reaction of this antacid with stomach acid. [3]

....

(c) What is the purpose of the two additives? [2]

Dimethicone: ....

....

The alginate: ....

....

Q3 (a) What is an analgesic? [1]

....

The two molecules below, A and B, are analgesics regularly used in medicine.

A: B:

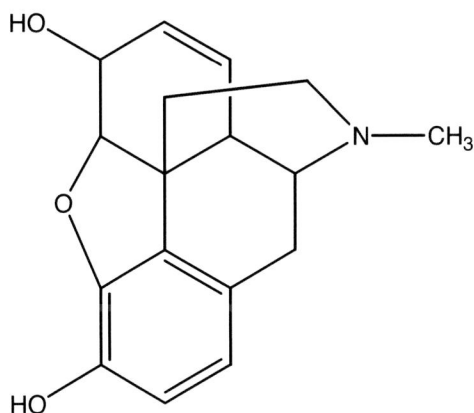
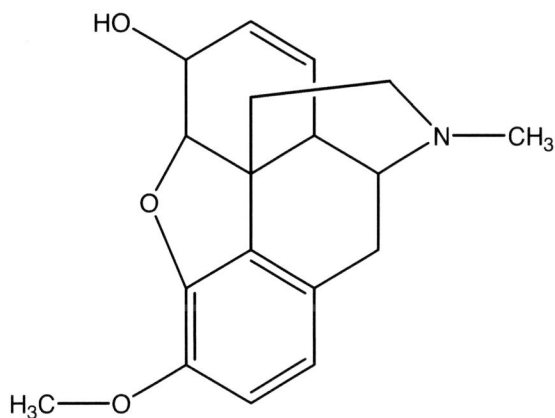

(b) To which class of analgesics do these molecules belong? [1]

....

(c) Briefly explain how these molecules may work, once in the body. [2]

....

....

....

(d) Molecule B differs from A in only one respect. Ring the group which is different on the diagram of B and name it below. [2]

....

Molecule C is a third analgesic, often used in the home as an alternative to aspirin.

C:

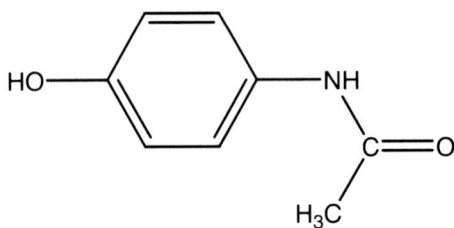

(e) Identify molcule C and give one advantage it has over aspirin. Give one disadvantage of the drug.   [3]

Identity: ……………………………………………………………………………………..

Advantage: …………………………………………………………………………………...

Disadvantage: ……………………………………………………………………………….

(f) How does its place of action differ from molecules A and B?   [1]

……………………………………………………………………………………………..

Q4 Ethanol can be thought of as a depressant.

(a) In the box, draw the structure of an ethanol molecule: [1]

(b) Outline some of the social and economic effects of ethanol abuse.   [3]

………………………………………………………………………………………………..

………………………………………………………………………………………………..

………………………………………………………………………………………………..

………………………………………………………………………………………………..

(c) Describe how the physiological effects of ethanol vary with increasing concentration (do not worry about any figures). [3]

....

....

....

....

(d) Giving an example involving ethanol, describe what is meant by the *synergistic effect*.

[3]

....

....

....

....

(e) Name one other depressant. [1]

....

Q5 The human body can be attacked by both bacteria and viruses and drugs have been developed to combat both.

(a) By using the differences between viruses and bacteria explain why it has been so much harder to develop anti-viral drugs than anti-bacterial ones. [3]

....

....

....

....

(b) Identify one anti-bacterial drug and outline how it works. [3]

....

....

....

....

(c) Identify one anti-viral drug and outline how it works. [3]

....

....

....

....

Questions for HL only

Q5 Describe what you understand by the each of the following.

(a) Chiral Auxiliary   [2]

....

....

....

(b) Combinatorial Library   [2]

....

....

....

(c) Broad Spectrum Antibiotic   [2]

....

....

....

Q6 Outline the significance of the following drugs, ot parts of drugs

(a) Cisplatin (include a diagram in the box)   [3]

....

....

....

....

....

(b) Thalidomide (diagram not needed).   [2]

....

....

....

(c) Indole Ring (include a diagram in the box)   [3]

....

....

....

....

....

Q7 Identify the names of two mind altering drugs in common use apart from cannabis. Describe their physiological effects. Construct a balanced discussion for and against the legalisation of cannabis.   [10]

Q8 Explain, using diagrams where useful, how combinatorial chemistry can be used to manufacture polypeptides from individual amino acids. State any advantages that this technique has over more traditional methods.   [10]

Q9 Outline the historical development of penicillins. Describe the importance of the beta-lactam ring and how the molecules have been adapted since their discovery to overcome the problem of bacterial resistance. State and explain two ways in which we have used antibiotics that have contributed to the problems of bacterial resistance.   [10]

A note about the spelling of element **S**. Most of the world have been spelling the name of this element with an 'f' for years. However the Brits have been holding out against the forces of banal simplicity and been, quite correctly, using 'ph'. Alas, recently our defences were shattered and a directive sent out from London to join everyone else. Yeah....right.